# DROWNING IN COMFORT

ANDRE D. WOODS

DROWNING IN COMFORT
WRITTEN AND ARRANGED BY:
ANDRE D. WOODS/ANDRE DOMINGO
ALL RIGHTS RESERVED.

NO PART OF THIS PUBLICATION MAY BE REPRODUCED,
DISTRIBUTED, OR TRANSMITTED IN ANY FORM OR BY ANY MEANS,
INCLUDING PHOTOCOPYING, RECORDING, OR OTHER ELECTRONIC
OR MECHANICAL METHODS, WITHOUT THE PRIOR WRITTEN
PERMISSION OF THE AUTHOR OR PUBLISHER

COVER ART AND DESIGN BY
RYAN A. WRIGHT


COPYRIGHT 2019© ANDRE D. WOODS/
ANDRE DOMINGO

# TABLE OF CONTENTS

- *8*   Introduction:
- *9*   Everywhere
- *10*   Observant
- *12*   Today
- *14*   Naive
- *15*   Backfire
- *18*   Enabled
- *19*   Holly Would
- *22*   Make Believe
- *24*   Razor Wings
- *25*   Evolution
- *27*   Buried Alive
- *29*   Moonshine
- *30*   Fall
- *31*   This Love Thing
- *33*   Her Style
- *34*   D.Y.E?
- *36*   Monster
- *37*   Scarifice
- *38*   Corruption
- *40*   Interview with The Past
- *45*   History
- *46*   Handle with Care
- *49*   You are not Alone...
- *50*   Universal Absence

51  Goodnight
53  Less=More
54  To Let It Be
55  Love Coward
57  Sinful Practice
58  Curiosity Kills
61  Car Rides
64  Warning
66  Picking Pedals
67  Even Exchange
69  Filters
71  One Night
73  Please (her)
75  Justice-ification
78  Instruments
79  Unsaid
80  Haunted
82  The Lengths
83  The Good Fight
85  Forever
86  First and Last
89  Soil
90  Repetition

*93* Authenticity
*94* Lifelines
*96* Caged Heart
*97* Te Amo
*98* Drowning in Comfort

# INTRODUCTION

"Too much comfort is poison,
It'll make the heart beat a consistent pace until it's numb...

Until the harm placed onto its essence is accepted.
Until the mind takes the wheel and the thought of starting over or moving on sends fear down the spine and you begin to live life on a flat line.

You think there isn't more.
You think it's all okay.

But okay is comfort's biggest ingredient; it is mediocrity...

It's deadly I tell you, to remain comfortably in pain."

## EVERYWHERE

I tell you I love you, not for you to hear...

I wish for the words to jump from the tip of my tongue and crawl upon your spine.
For your skin to show braille of every reason why.
For the hairs upon your neck to ignite like candle flames.
For the temperature between your legs to raise with the sunrise, as the heart melts and leaks into your desirability.

Hear me if you must.

But feel me my dear.... *everywhere.*

## OBSERVANT

Pay your attention closely to the gestures.

When the insecurities one hides, begin to form into their cell phone screen.

When "I'm outside to say goodnight", turn into facetimes... facetimes turn into phone calls... phone calls turn into text messages and "goodnight" turns into question marks before a sleepless night.

It is a gift and a curse, to be observant. Everything you see is enhanced by the soul. The little things are monuments inside one's heart. They live inside the reasonless smile after the eyes dance with the music inside car rides. They breathe within the relaxation of the eyes as the fingertips are gliding along the hairs on the back of the neck.

The little things, we must always see.
But we mustn't be naive. When the little things begin to open our eyes to a place we wish never, to vision.

## TODAY

With mascara smeared around her eyes and a wrinkled bouquet of roses wrapped in her arm, she stood there... hands shaking as the rose petals released and descended to the sidewalk much like broken promises. She never knew how to let go of the things she knew would one day leave her empty handed.

As the moment fades into yesterday, she continues to look forward to... today.

"You wanted depth and you've let me drown in my very own vulnerability.

I wish it upon no one... to fight, keeping their neck above a shallow heart."

## NAIVE

To say I'd never hurt you would be a lie my love. If anyone promises you a painless love, run the other way. There will be days when you will cry and I will soak myself in every tear, until learning lessons hydrate my foolishness.

I will unwillingly hurt you. But it will become a second nature to heal you my dear... and it will never be for the same reason.

In these times your smile will become a means of survival...

As water is for the body.
As blood is for the heart.
As peace is for the mind.

As you are.... for I.

## BACK FIRE

When should the trying surrender?

I've heard them say it is
when the effort becomes
self inflicting... when your
arms are open and the
space between begins to eat
the very meat from your rib
cage. When an
unanswered phone call
shape shifts into the feeling
of an unreciprocated "I love you."

Should it be easier to hold
on then to let go?... I've
dreamt premonitions of
you and I winning this war,
but I've had nightmares of
the war being between you

and I my dear.
I no longer want our hearts
to live like swords and our
minds to be the shields.
Our words were poetry
and now, nuclear warfare
ignites at the dot after
every sentence.

The questions hurt much
more than they used to...
Is this just a battle we've lost?

Have we lost one another?
...Or will we live to fight
another day?
"I will love you until I die...",
we've said once before.
I've never wished
death to be so literal.

As our hearts beat and beat
and beat. When will the
beating stop?

I hope these questions
never come with an answer...
I only want this page to be
poetry... and nothing more.

## ENABLED

Your smile is my happiness.
Your humor is my laughter.
Your moan is my pleasure.
Your warmth is my comfort.
Your orgasm is my climax.
Your open mind is my vision.
Your passion is my goal.
Your free spirit is my wings.
Your soul is my oxygen.

Stay with me...
Your existence is life amongst my universe.

## HOLLY WOULD

She walked into my
apartment with the smell
of Hollywood dancing
from her dress. Her heels
dangling from her finger
tips as her eyes descended
slowly within every blink.

                I used to love her before
                the city did. Before her
                pupils dilated into the
                lights. Before every goose
                bump I gave her turned
                into a bunch of likes...
                When her favorite view
                stood above Mulholland
                drive, opposed to the
                numbers below every
                video she posted.

We used to slow dance in
empty rooms without
music and listen to the
voice of our energy sing
songs we said we'd never forget.

There she was, at 2:00am
mumbling a song I was
unaware of...

I looked her in the eyes
and vacancy was all I
could reminisce...
"I missed you..." she said.
As I replied, "I still miss you...".

Her mind didn't put the
words together. Her heart
was just going through the
motions. Her hands began

to slip the strap of her
dress down each shoulder.
As she stood and hugged
me with nothing on.

She was naked, but all I
could see was the layers...
She was somewhere in
there and she wanted me
to find her. Little did she
know I was lost inside the
same place... as I was only
trying to find where I've gone...
Just lost inside the city...

## MAKE BELIEVE

Let us pretend our blood becomes warmer when our bodies curl into one.
Let us pretend we are still blind and we do not see indifference opening its arms to what we've made.

The making of love no longer comes with the kiss.
Our sweat is now something we think of in the midst of every moan. We are feeding off lust my dear.

We used to lay our spirits along the present. As the hands of time caressed our spines and now it is the present in which we use to scavenge for tomorrow.

Let us pretend there is not a silent "I miss you..." in every "I love you..."

Let's play make believe.... until we no longer have any belief to make...

## RAZOR WINGS

At times the air is sharp...

Every inhale invites a razor to trickle down your stomach and dance along the wings of the butterflies fighting to stay alive.

If you could only save the butterflies...
But when the oxygen turns against you...
It is evident...

It was just not meant to be.

## EVOLUTION

I knew it was bad news.
She thought she could change me... help me grow...
and she did.

But she wasn't ready for the man she evolved me
to be.

She never thought I'd be the person she always
wanted. She never even got to love what she
made. She was a hard worker, but that's all she
really was.

*"It was much like the wind instigating a wild fire...*
*The way she moved on."*

## BURIED ALIVE

Though the soul can last forever, it can evaporate slowly behind circumstance... and all that will be left behind are unreciprocated cries to the shadows, blank stares through picture perfect sceneries...

The eyes will close at night and wait for a dream to play, only to wake and see morning... and then there will be a human next to you... something you used to call love but only sees you as a circumstance...

A soul buried alive.

*"As bad as it sounds, I'd have more peace of mind if I knew you felt the same emptiness I do."*

## MOONSHINE

She was a Mixture of noon and midnight...
and as we made lust out of love, she showed me
what the sun and the moon have in common... the
ability to make me feel as if I was the only one she
shined for at that very moment.

She made it okay, to be a fool.

## FALL

Maybe it is the leaves we follow. They grow upon the trees in solitude until they are ready to descend. If only our hearts were built to be pure.

To be raised by the sun and water.

We wouldn't have to wait until the sunrays begin to weaken to fall.

The leaves drop
The sun drops
The temperature drops
The rain drops...

and our hearts begin to follow...

Until we are ready to Fall.

## THIS LOVE THING

Maybe some of us were created for the muddle it
offers, this love thing.
Falling
in and out
then back in again...
Our passion shifts as if our hearts mold onto
the bow of an insane violinist, playing the genius
sounds of our chaotic rhythms.

We carry amusement parks in our souls, with
roller coasters built by the very hands we hold
onto.
Maybe we were made to love like goddamn gas
prices... something we have no control of, but we
need and pump inside the engines of our vessels.

The ups and downs keep us alive.
There's no right way to do it.

ANDRE D. WOODS

...This love thing.

## HER STYLE

There was a style to the way she danced in the dark. She laid back upon the bed as if her soul became the sheets of my mattress...The way she opened her legs slowly, just as the sun ascends and teases the ocean. Her fingertips gliding upon her skin, while the air persuaded her limbs.

There was a style, a grace to her temptation. Just as a swaying flame is lit upon the wick of a candle. She took all the attention away from the shadows... and when she melted my soul insid her fire, she did it... with style.

## D.Y.E?

"Did you eat?", she would ask.
One of those questions you never pay attention to until you're hungry and she is at home wiping tear drops from her bedroom vanity...

She always cleaned me up, dug the dirt from my fingernails, licked her thumb and wiped the bit of make up she left from randomized gestures of love from her lips to my cheek.

She was made of the simplest things, much like Mother Earth, a heart purified by the sea. Her eyes were made of the galaxies. Her skin was planted of seeds blossoming from her aura and growing into the garden of Eden. Exhaling oxygen that always seem to keep me alive...

...and even though I ripped the butterflies from her stomach until it was vacant of her very own appetite, she still sat there along her vanity, lights dim and a face full of smeared make up... just wondering, if I had anything to eat...

"Did you eat?", she would ask... but I always wanted more.

## MONSTER

You must fight at times.
There must be a battle until love becomes unnoticed.

Every now and then, you must shove love under the bed and let your desires burn within the friction of the skin until you are scarred by lust.

Scare the shadows into the corners with her screams and force the walls of the bedroom to look the other way.

Sometimes love is not enough and you have to shake things up a little.

Until you realize how much you both enjoy the monsters within.

## SCARIFICE

If you begin to drown in the shallow depths of this world, I'll auction off my last breath to the desperation of your lungs. Sit with you on roller coasters of your broken heart, until the wheels fall off and we lay face first on the pavement of every moment vandalizing the buildings along your memory lane.

I may not stop the pain or even bring it to ease... but I will gather scars with you and loneliness will never be one.

## CORRUPTION

She was the home of innocence, this girl.
Her presence was of a goddess within a place of mediocrity. Her waist stood slim above hips that kissed the wind beside her as she walked. She was merely the closest living thing to perfection.

I remember we sat along the Westwood streets, exchanging questions at ease, conversing as if our words were oxygen for our lungs. She would graze my hand long enough to let me know she was here to stay, but only if I knew how to hold on. She was good... so good even I could not stand to be inside my skin when I began to touch her.

Being inside her would be much like vandalizing a church or spitting on a newly painted white wall. Although I yearned for her innocence... I'd never commit corruption to her soul.

These palms of mine are not meant to hold clean hands...Holy water does not chase well with Hennessy.

ANDRE D. WOODS

## INTERVIEW WITH THE PAST

Interviewer – "What's your
take on love Mr. Woods?

       As I replied with laughter
       in my eyes....

"You want to know
the truth about love?

It's a beautiful thing...

Ocean waves endings
kissing the start of the shore.
Gentle gusts of wind on
warm sunny days.
Raindrops placed along
fallen leaves...
...all that good stuff...
But like any gift from

Mother Nature, it holds a
side of calamity, natural disasters.
hurricanes,
tsunamis,
desert storms… It changes you…

When agony carves
someone else's name along
the inside of your ribcage.
When loneliness poisons
lightless rooms with the
last exhale in goodbye.
When you drink liquor
from your very own glass
heart until it is empty,
just waiting to be dropped
and shattered by the
belligerent hands of indifference.

You want the truth?
I hope you've cried every

tear I've caged behind the
bloodshot bars in my eyes.
I hope you are haunted by
the person you used to be.

I hope your bed sheets tell
you how much they miss
me when the wind wakes
you in the middle of the
night and reminds you,
alone is not enough.

You give someone the
world and once they are
gone, the world becomes
vacant. You do everything
with them and suddenly,
all is just a reminder of nothing.
...that is right, nothing!

Forever becomes figment.

Never becomes now.
Scratches become scars.
Tongues turn into weapons.
I turn to you, you turn away
and love becomes something
you used to be. You want the goddamn truth?

I hope your heart beats my
favorite song until you can
hear my happiness trapped
inside your historic love.
Until you feel spiteful enough to
hope I feel the same miserable way.

There's a truth inside the
madness, it's rotten and
it's raw, it's harsh, but it's
real and it's the only way
I will know before this
disaster, we were once
something...

Beautiful.
I don't not want revenge, I
just for once want to
know you and I both.
Feel... This.
You want to know the truth huh?"
But I was never sure if the truth
hurt me or her more...

## HISTORY

Her skin was made out of
ease, with a voice sung by
sounded winds and ocean
waves singing over the shore...
I fount infinity in her eyes
and felt the future along
the tip of her swaying fingers.
She knew how to tell the story
without ever mentioning the end...
the moments we fool ourselves
away from, and then tomorrow
 comes around and her fairy tale
suddenly turns into yesterday.

## HANDLE WITH CARE

I can see the way I hurt you.
Shattered mirrors
compliment the cracks of
your bloodshot eyes,
reflecting on the agony
looking straight into mine.

Broken glass cannot be
repaired back to its
original state, my love.
But as I gather the pieces
with blood on my
fingertips, I will pinpoint
the beauty within each
shard, hoping to rebuild a
reflection of something far
more than the mess I've made.
I can see the way I've hurt
you my dear.

But I can feel it much more
 and with shaky hands I
will clean up the
catastrophe I've caused.

*"...and the twisted truth about reality is... sometimes it is meant to be...and it still doesn't..."*

## YOU ARE NOT ALONE

The memories infiltrating your mind are our creations. Every laugh and every heartache was mixed together with the hands we once held. So when you look back and see me... just know I too, look back and see you... and even when you are sitting with your head down and a fistful of tears... Remember mine too, are infused with every drop. As I sit here in hopes you know we are sharing the same daydream... even though it feels much like a nightmare.

You are not alone. It is me in there.

Keep me alive.

## UNIVERSAL ABSENCE

I know it hurts my dear, I feel it too.
There is an agony using my stomach as a jungle gym

Empty inhales and pointless exhales.

Pain locked inside my ribcage.
Memories floating in the mind behind the drop of each tear.

I've gotten so used to your love.
My skin waits for your touch.
My bed sheets reach for your scent.
The sun rays shine through my
windows without purpose in the morning.

I know it hurts... to be without love.
You were my everything and now everything is just something without you.

## GOODNIGHT

Once we ripped the dark into pieces, we laid there.

Her head rested over my racing heart, my legs laid underneath her shaken thigh... as she traced every scratch she made along my neck and shoulders as I fit my hand inside the welt I made upon the perfection behind her.

We laid there and caressed the mess we made of each other until we surrendered in our sleep.

It was our way of saying "Goodnight".

*"...and maybe love is just an illusion and we are all just much to eager to be fooled.*

*Addicted to dreams, we all are... or just much too fearful of the reality of never feeling felt."*

## LESS = MORE

That's all it takes, that little piece of hope.

Just a small piece to keep the pain around a little longer.

It's the process... that's how it goes.

The hope keeps it alive until it turns on you slowly and becomes humiliation.

It's the hope.

Although it gives life, it has a small taste of death within its expiration.

## TO LET IT BE

You will kill yourself seeking for the right time to let go, scavenging for the answers.

Sometimes the fire in these cold hearts of ours die down and the only thing to reignite your soul is the solitude that awaits.

## LOVE COWARD

Ease is not love.
Challenge is not love.

It dances between the lines of the wretched and the nostalgic.

We speak of the good when the hearts begin to bleed, and then fear the repetition of the bad when our ribcages secure us within our warmth.

A bunch of contradictive humans, we are.
We only see love when it is gone and we dissect it down to every flaw when love makes its attempt to embrace our existence.

A bunch of love cowards, this generation has become. Asking for others advice with tears smeared upon our eyelids. The feeling is the only thing we have to keep for ourselves in this self serving world... ...

we cannot choose when we wish others to understand our fires and then shun them in between I love you.

## SINFUL PRACTICE

Never allow your love to be anything short of admired...

If it is, and you feel the left over love rotting inside your chest before you sleep, do not accept it.
Let it settle.
Let it hurt.
But once it hits rock bottom...
Let it go.

Your passion mustn't remain within the unappreciative soul.

But it must learn the torture to overcome and evolve.

Do not settle.

Settling is a practice of hate.

## CURIOSITY KILLS

We are both gone.

Apart.

Just two numb,
crippled, blind
individuals
searching for a
purpose… with
our eyes up, legs
standing and arms out.

Keeping our necks
above the surface
of "I miss you."
Wondering if it is
just the process of
letting go or a
reminder to try

again every time
we feel the absence
poisoning every inhale.

The course of
heartbreak is a fine
line wrapping
around our vessels
and it cuts the
circulation from
the feeling.
We begin to lose sight
of our intuition and
we are forced to
make decisions
off of theories.

I wonder if you are numb.
If you are, I wonder if it means
we are still aligned.

I wonder if this is
the development of
our unfolding.


If this is the end, I
beg the universe to
give you
everything I couldn't...


and if it is not...


I hope this is the
beginning of a
universe I can provide.

## CAR RIDES

We drove home.

It was just another day
spending quality time.
But much like the car we
drove, the value
depreciates with every mile.

We used to get lost in
music and sing old school
songs until one of our
vocal chords collapsed
and the other would pick up
the slack. Everything
was a reflection of our love.

She would do things to
distract me from the road
just to show me how much

she'd risk to cease the
moment of a simple car
ride with me...
...and there we were...
All I could hear was the
gravel underneath the
constantly spinning tires.
The air condition blew into
every inhale, just to
remind everything inside
me the warmth was
no longer there.

Just her and I, existing
inside the silence.

I stopped in front of her
apartment.
She kissed me goodbye.
With our vocal chords as
strong as ever we said,

## DROWNING IN COMFORT

- "I love you."
- "I love you too."

and the door closed.

Just spending some *quality time.*

## WARNING

It may be a while...
Until this heart of mine can contribute to that glass of yours my dear.

I have found my soul inside the darkest places these days and the bit of light I have only seems to brighten a small box I am fighting to escape.

I can see your open hands grasping to pull me out and the more you reach, the more I can feel you entering this place you do not deserve.

I can feel your finger tips grazing my skin. Your eyes are peaking in and I smile just to make sure my appreciation travels to you, but I cannot move. There is no gesture in my love for you.

My blood is turning cold and there is nothing outside of me to grant me fire. I wish for you not to leave, but I'd never bring it upon you to stay.

I am not sure if I am trapped inside your heart or my very own mind, but the story will end the same... I have to break out of this place I'm in, my dear... it will be my closest feeling to death...

and that is no place for you.

## PICKING PEDALS

"Until death do us part", we speak.

Maybe we are not looking for someone to love until we die... more so, we all seem to be looking for someone to be in love with while we die.

She loves me...
She loves me not...

As the pedals drop much like the days going away.

## EVEN EXCHANGE

Without my hands,
                                      I'd like to touch
you.
Without my tongue,
                                      I'd like to taste
you.
Without you standing,
                                      I'd like to make you
come.
Without my mind,
                                      I'd like to know
you.
Without my presence,
                                      I'd like to be there.

Without my heart, I could do all these things.

Give me yours and I'll give you mine.

ANDRE D. WOODS

"We will go outside of ourselves fighting to keep love alive or to dodge heartbreak.

But we never distinguish which one it really is."

## FILTERS

She was the filter I needed...
Even on my darkest days, she brought brightness to the pictures I painted to make my soul remember the masterpiece within me.

Every scar embedded under the layers of my skin were brushed away, with strokes of her hands swaying along my tattoos. It was her way of showing praise to my entirety, even though I chose to place the painful ink upon myself.

I'd go days without sleep, and the hands of the night would scribble red lines along my eyes and place below them the very pillows I neglected. But with the purity of her pearly eyes she'd stare at me until I dreamt inside her pupils... it was the closest I got to sleep and I felt alive.

No matter how I felt... ...

No matter how I looked.

Her presence enhanced my existence.

There wasn't an app in the world that could replace her.
There wasn't a filter in need...

## ONE NIGHT

She left a good taste in my mouth.
The Flavors of life, she possessed.

My tongue tiptoed along her perfume until it became the natural scent of temptation.
Her liquor infused saliva swam through my gums as my words began to drown.
My mouth grazed along her unspoken lips along with my fingertips.
I moved my head to the side, and allowed my teeth to grip the shaken vulnerabilities of her inner thigh.
She was my favorite flavor and to this day I can still taste her somewhere inside my soul.

Life changing, she was... and she only needed a Saturday night.

"The only thing worse than fighting to go back in time, is fighting to bring the past forward. As you drag your pain to those in your present."

## PLEASE (HER)

At times you have to
make infinite love to her.

Until the legs can no longer shake
and she moans until
her voice is lost
somewhere inside the shadows.

Until the bed surrenders
and the sheets descend
to the floor like a
lopsided boxing match.

Until she gives up
on lust for the
evening.

Every now and then
you have to ware it out

even if you do not finish.

To let her know at times...
...It's all about her.

## JUSTICE-IFICATION

I am convinced, humans are placed in front of other humans for a reason. But I am also convinced these reasons mustn't be known all the time. The process of life revolves around the cycle of contradiction...

Finding the medium of love and logic.
Allowing our minds to take the wheel of our hearts. Giving other humans the control of our intuition.

So here I am
one me minus one you...

In reality, it just equals one
me without one you.
But within me, I am absent
and you have taken me
with you. The feeling
I have exerted to extract
from you has gone missing...

So I am convinced...

Maybe I was here to show
you the feeling still exists
in that vacant soul you've
kept boarded up for so long.
All you needed was a
dreamer to cover your eyes
and make you believe the
feeling can be infused
with permanence.
I've never been good with
oblivion my dear.

## DROWNING IN COMFORT

I have seen far too much in
very little time.
Just a victim of life's
contradiction.

## INSTRUMENTS

The Body is art and desire
is the secret ingredient
to its awakening.
Therapeutic music we
presumed it to be.
The limbs, the organs,
the hidden keys become
instruments and mine
symphonized within hers
until her voice harmonized
with my madness…and
between her moans was
my amnesia. As I have
forgotten what
life was like…
before she came around,
over and over again.

## UNSAID

Satisfaction mustn't always be said.
Pay close attention.

It is when you feel the weight of her head rest fully against your chest, or the fingers begin to curl lighter as the hand is held. When her legs tremble upon your shoulders or the nails draw the thoughts behind her every moan upon the skin on your back.

Those are the moments when satisfaction kisses your soul with appreciation.

Without a word to be said.

## HAUNTED

That pain in your soul you feel…

As if love is clawing its way out of your mouth through every exhale…

When hands of every care in the world you've ever given, wraps around your neck and pulls your mind into flashbacks of misplaced nostalgia and your dreams begin to play hide and seek with your pillowcase.

That feeling is not weakness and you mustn't become fooled by its scheme to go back.

Do not let agony take you away from solitude or trick you into resurrecting a love who killed you once before.

*"What will I be without them?"*

*You ask yourself.*

*The answer is quite simple.*

*You will be You.*

## THE LENGTHS

I've given you more love than I've been taught to give my dear. My beating muscle, it beats heavier than the bones of my ribcage can sustain and my soul…it has built a world with the tools to build a home, all within you.

There is a debt in my heart and I've overspent my existence for you. Yet alive, I still feel.

All is possible, but only with you.

## THE GOOD FIGHT

We fought to fight.
We fought to love.
We fought to agree.
We fought to disagree.
We fought to stay.
We fought to leave.
We fought to feel.

We fought to let go. It was the hardest battle we ever faced. She would say "goodbye" and I would ask "how". I would walk away and she would splash the bit of love she had left in her tank along with the very shoes I stepped in.

It's a fight that never seems to end - when it all ends. Yet we always find a way to fight the good fight once again.

All it took was, "I miss you, my love".

ANDRE D. WOODS

We fought a lot, her and I.

I am not sure if I ever want it to stop.

## FOREVER

Please don't speak the words forever, my dear. I have not a clue what it means. When the syllables begin to flow from the flip of your bottom lip it still seems to invade my imagination, just as art should. There is a foolish hope who dances inside my soul... a ballerina with perfect feet and she twirls inside the lifeless halls within me and those are the places I need, to stay here on earth. Forever does not exist and still I write poetry that never ends and it always seems to be about you. I do not know if it is because I wish to believe in this fallacy or if I wish to believe you yearn for my existence for such a time. Forever is more harmful than love. Some of us forget love inside forever and it is a slow death.

Just love me now, every day. Though, forever sounds quite nice... it is not always the case.

ANDRE D. WOODS

## FIRST AND LAST

She cried in front of me.
It wasn't the first time.
Usually my reflex is to
consult her.
Even if I was the reason
she ached, I found a way
to dance with her along
the medium until peace
flooded her veins.

But this time around, I did
not reach to meet
halfway... as her tears fell
from her cheek and landed
onto the cold-hardwood
floor of my bedroom.
Her bloodshot eyes made
lines of endless question
marks and the only
answer I had sat

somewhere along the
voice of the silence.
Much like the sound of
the very end of
a war full of
lifeless casualties.
Our souls were unaligned.

        It hurt me to watch her cry.
        Unaware if the pain was
        rooted from seeing a
        woman I loved suffer, or
        the realism of the white
        flags wrapped around my neck.

        I always feared death to be this
        way...
        A slow unanswered agony
        without cause and effect.
        A life without feeling.

She cried in front of me.

It wasn't the first time.

I too, cried inside.

I didn't know it at the time.

But I know now…

I just had to wait until she was gone.

## SOIL

I must caress every ripple amongst your rock bottom. Meditate inside the cold, shadowy corners of your soul's abode and find comfort inside the thoughts turning your body, while you go to war with your sleep. The benefits do not only sit within the music of your laughter and the frame of your smile, my dear.

It is the chaos raining upon your filthy soil before you blossom... it is that, I yearn for.

# REPETITION

"I Love You..."

"I Love You too..."

"I Miss You..."

"I Miss You too..."

                    A kiss goodnight... night after night, until the moon and the stars begin to dim more and more along with the point of it all... A kiss goodnight until the lips fall numb to the feeling.

Inside the stomach lives one little butterfly. It stands alone waiting to be reunited with the moments it once fluttered with. The wings, they feed

from spontaneity and chaos.
It is an empty feeling, to feel a single
butterfly drifting within
you with broken wings
and nobody else to
celebrate with. Unsure,
whether or not the feeling
is still a sign of hope or a
symbol of surrender.

So we say it again,
"I Love You...",
... waiting desperately
for the butterflies to swarm...

        Buts there's only one...
        Dying slowly as it breathes
        the same air we once
        called Love...

"I Miss You..."

ANDRE D. WOODS

...as the butterfly finally

floats over my head...

luckily you are no longer here...

because I mean it now...

but it is not meant for you to hear.

## AUTHENTICITY

We ripped the dark into pieces and laid there...

                          Her head rested
                          over my racing heart.

                          My legs laid
                          underneath her
                          shaken thigh.

As she traced every scratch she created along my neck to my shoulders blades and I fit my hand perfectly inside the masterpiece I made upon her perfect behind.

We laid there... and caressed the mess we made of one another until we surrendered into our sleep. It was our way of saying goodnight and we said it differently every time.

## LIFELINES

My tongue rode her spine and felt the ups and downs.
She sat above my existence, as I felt her ups and downs.
I alternated the kiss of both set of her lips, until she felt my ups and downs.
Her nails drug along my tattoos as she felt my ups and downs.

Up and down
Up and down.

It was the lifeline of our love... as we lived through ups and downs.

"We live in a time where letting go requires much
more heart than falling in love...

Leaving us with less than what we started."

## CAGED HEART

She was a dove and my
heart was a cage...

...and when I let her go, she learned to fly... as I
learned to open my soul.

There was much more to
her than me and much
more to me than her, and
pain was the only way
we'd know.

Bittersweet, it is.

I wish I could thank her for leaving me, as I hope
she'd say the same for letting her go.

## TE AMO

"I do love you..."
As the silence swam within our lungs and the discomfort laid between our fingertips.

I felt fear drumming its beat along our hearts and it was then, I knew... forever had taken its role.

Control was gone.

She looked me in the eyes, whiskey stained along each exhale, and she captured me.

It was the first time I saw forever in the flesh.
It was the first time I saw the beauty in death.
It was the first time I questioned the next step.

She was a page in a book I've written...
But when I spoke of love, I then became a page behind.

...cheers, my dear...to your victory.

Be careful around those who are imprisoned by the average love. They will tell you the fire will stop burning inside the soul and the nails will no longer engrave symbols of passion onto the skin. They will speak of crazy people as if sanity exists. The ones who never cry of pain or laughter. Be cautious of the normal love. It will only make you sane and drive you to mediocrity.

Do not swim with those who only wish to float. They are only...

## Drowning in Comfort...

DROWNING IN COMFORT

ANDRE D. WOODS

www.ingramcontent.com/pod-product-compliance
Lightning Source LLC
Chambersburg PA
CBHW021957290426
44108CB00012B/1111